"The Effects on Reading Proficiency

元认知监控理论下的
初中英语阅读实效性研究

for Junior Middle School Students
—— From the Perspective of Metacognitive Regulation Training"

胡萍 著

图书在版编目（CIP）数据

元认知监控理论下的初中英语阅读实效性研究＝The Effects on Reading Proficiency for Junior Middle School Students: From the Perspective of Metacognitive Regulation Training: 汉英对照 / 胡萍著. —成都：西南交通大学出版社，2017.1
ISBN 978-7-5643-5159-5

Ⅰ. ①元… Ⅱ. ①胡… Ⅲ. ①英语－阅读教学－教学研究－初中 Ⅳ. ①G633.412

中国版本图书馆 CIP 数据核字（2016）第 290057 号

元认知监控理论下的初中英语阅读实效性研究
The Effects on Reading Proficiency for Junior Middle School Students: From the Perspective of Metacognitive Regulation Training

胡萍 著

责任编辑	赵玉婷
助理编辑	孟 媛
封面设计	严春艳
出版发行	西南交通大学出版社 （四川省成都市二环路北一段 111 号 西南交通大学创新大厦 21 楼）
发行部电话	028-87600564　028-87600533
邮政编码	610031
网　　址	http://www.xnjdcbs.com
印　　刷	成都中铁二局永经堂印务有限责任公司
成品尺寸	165 mm × 230 mm
印　　张	5.75
字　　数	107 千
版　　次	2017 年 1 月第 1 版
印　　次	2017 年 1 月第 1 次
书　　号	ISBN 978-7-5643-5159-5
定　　价	25.00 元

图书如有印装质量问题　本社负责退换
版权所有　盗版必究　举报电话：028-87600562

Preface

As one of the most basic language skills, reading has become a new indispensable way to acquire knowledge and information of science and technology. How to improve students', reading level has been one of the focal points of foreign language teaching. Metacognitive self-regulation is a strategy as well as an effective way which is used to guide and help the readers to adjust and control the reading process in terms of psychology, so as to cultivate students' reading ability. This book is an empirical study about the relationship between metacognitive self-regulation training and English reading among junior middle school students. Having known the reading comprehension ability and the use of the metacognitive self-regulation of the students, the teachers adopt some training methods which are based on strategies for foreign language teaching , then teach the students and make them master the the strategy of metacognitive self-regulation, revealing the relationship between metacognitive self-regulation strategies and English reading learning. All is to provide important basis and enlightenment for the research on English reading comprehension for the junior middle school students, the training of metacognitive self-regulation and EFL teaching.

The book consists of the following six chapters.

Chapter one is an introduction that gives a brief background of the research concerning with this topic, the significance of the study and the structure of the book.

Chapter two presents a literature review, which examines the recent studies on metacognition and reciprocal teaching. And focuses on the theoretical bases which consists of two parts: part one introduces the theories concerning reading; part two introduces the relevant theories of reading strategy and its supportive language teaching theories.

Chapter three introduces the methodology employed in the research, which includes research questions, subjects, instruments, methods and procedure.

Chapter four, experimental implementation, describes what is going on during the ten weeks in detail.

Chapter five, data collection and analysis, provides detailed analyses of the data collected. The reasons for the findings are discussed and the pedagogical implications are also suggested.

In Chapter six, the conclusion is drawn, the limitations of the research are suggested and directions for future research in this regard are recommended.

The subjects involved in the study are 120 students from Grade Two in Zhaotong Experimental Middle School. Having known their reading comprehension ability and the use of the metacognitive self-regulation by using the questionnaire, the target group received reading instruction by using the metacognitive self-regulation training method for 10 weeks. The result of the training is as the following:

First, although reading instruction with reciprocal teaching brought some positive effects to the target group on their test performance, the difference was not statistically significant enough. But there is quite difference in the use of some metacognitive self-regulation strategies.

Second, the analysis of the scores of some typical comprehension questions found that the target group got significant higher mark than the controlled group, the strategies included guessing word meanings from the context and scanning for specific information. This finding shows that reading instruction with reciprocal teaching really enhances students' awareness of reading strategy employment and the use of some strategies has become automatic in solving comprehension problems.

Because of the complexity of using strategy and the process of reading, it is so hard to avoid some deficiency in terms of concept, methods and some other aspect, and these findings in this thesis still need to be verified in the future research.

Contents

Chapter One Introduction 1

    1.1   Research Background 1

    1.2   The Significance of the Study 3

    1.3   The Structure of the Book 3

Chapter Two Literature Review 5

    2.1   Metacognition 5

        2.1.1   The history of metacognition 5

        2.1.2   Metacognition and learning 10

        2.1.3   Scaffolded instruction 11

    2.2   Reading 13

        2.2.1   Defining reading 13

        2.2.2   Models of reading 14

        2.2.3   Defining reading strategy 15

        2.2.4   The classification of reading strategies 16

        2.2.5   Comprehensible input 19

2.3   Research on Metacognition Concerning Reading in China   20

2.4   Reciprocal Teaching   21

Chapter Three   Methodology   26

3.1   Research Questions   26

3.2   Subjects   27

3.3   Instruments   28

    3.3.1   Questionnaire   28

    3.3.2   Experimental tests   29

3.4   Methods   30

3.5   Procedures   31

    3.5.1   Taking pre-test   32

    3.5.2   Instructions with two models   32

    3.5.3   Taking post-test and filling in questionnaire   33

    3.5.4   Data collection and analysis   33

Chapter Four   Experimental Instruction   34

4.1   Instruction to the Controlled Group   35

4.2   Instruction to the Target Group   37

Chapter Five   Data Analysis and Result   44

5.1   Analysis of the Pre-test and Discussion on the Results   44

             5.1.1   Analysis of the pre-test   44

             5.1.2   Discussion   45

   5.2   Analysis of the Questionnaire and Discussion on the Results   46

             5.2.1   Analysis of the general means of the two groups   47

             5.2.2   Analysis of the means of each questionnaire item   48

             5.2.3   Discussion   51

   5.3   Analysis of the Post-test and Discussion on the Results   56

             5.3.1   Analysis of the difference between the two groups in the post-test   56

             5.3.2   Discussion   56

             5.3.3   Analysis of the difference in some individual comprehension items between the two groups   58

             5.3.4   Discussion   60

   5.4   Pedagogical Implication   61

Chapter Six   Conclusion   64

References   68

Appendix 1   73

Appendix 2   76

Appendix 3   78

Postscript   80

Chapter One

Introduction

1.1 Research Background

It is encouraging to see that the research into language learning strategy has focused on determining successful and unsuccessful strategies for language improvement in China (Wen & Johnson, 1997:27). However, "the available research into PRC EFL learners is disproportionate with the country's foreign language needs" (Zhang, 2001:268). Even sparse is the available research into Chinese junior middle school English learners. In order to clarify the current interest in junior middle school EFL reading research in China, the author of this thesis browsed the degree papers and academic papers published since the year of 2002 to now in Wan Fang Data by the key words "metacognition", "reading" and "middle school" in an effort to find out the research interest in China's middle school EFL reading research. Of the about 50 papers that are suitable for the key words, 18 papers deal with junior middle school EFL teaching, and only 6 papers investigate the correlation between metacognitive strategy training and reading instruction, which shows that the research dealing with junior middle school EFL reading instruction with metacognition training is far from being enough to reveal the real picture in this aspect and it seems that in junior middle school EFL reading instruction, metacognition training has not aroused enough attention.

In 2003, Ministry of Education of the PRC published *Full-time Middle School English Course Teaching Standard (on Trial)* to reform middle school EFL teaching and its curriculum design. It stipulates the EFL reading proficiency for students of each grade in middle school and emphasizes the integration of learning strategy training into classroom teaching practice, which challenges teachers to take advantage of more effective teaching methods and learning strategy training means to provide students with the teaching which enables students to develop in all aspects of English learning.

To meet the requirement set by the ministry, the author of the thesis designs the classroom teaching based on the theory of metacognitive self-regulation and the teaching practice of reciprocal teaching to investigate whether or not the explicit training of self-regulation during students' reading process can enable students to use reading strategies, especially metacognitive reading strategies, more successfully to handle problems while reading, and to find out if it is effective in improving students' reading comprehension in the context of junior middle school EFL reading lessons in China.

1.2 The Significance of the Study

As mentioned above, the training of metacognitive strategies and self-regulation while reading among Chinese junior middle school EFL students are not sufficient and the research in this area is too scarce to direct teaching practice. The present study aims at enriching the research in this field and providing more data for other EFL teachers' reference. If the research questions are answered satisfactorily at the end of the study, it will undoubtedly improve English teaching and facilitate English learning in the following ways:

(1) To help students become strategic-conscious EFL readers, to make students more systematic in their use of strategies, to enhance students' reading comprehension competence, and to build up autonomous learning ability;

(2) To explore and develop an English reading teaching mode in order to develop students' metacognitive regulation awareness and improve their reading performance.

1.3 The Structure of the Book

The book consists of the following six chapters.

Chapter one is an introduction that gives a brief background of the research concerning with this topic, the significance of the study and the thesis structure.

Chapter two presents a literature review, which examines the recent studies on metacognition and reciprocal teaching. And focuses on the theoretical bases which consists of two parts: part one introduces the theories concerning reading; part two introduces the relevant theories of reading strategy and its supportive language teaching theories.

Chapter three introduces the methodology employed in the research, which includes research questions, subjects, methods and procedure.

Chapter four, experimental implementation, describes what is going on during the ten weeks in detail.

Chapter five, data collection and analysis, provides detailed analyses of the data collected. The reasons for the findings are discussed and the pedagogical implications are also suggested.

In Chapter six, the conclusion is drawn, the limitations of the research are suggested and directions for future research in this regard are recommended.

Chapter Two

Literature Review

2.1 Metacognition

2.1.1 The history of metacognition

Before the word metacognition was coined, developmentalists such as Dewey and Piaget acknowledged that children learn by doing and by thinking about what they are doing in their studies about mental processes (Kirkpatrick, 1985:10). When Pólya (1957) developed his heuristics for problem solving, he was outlining ways for students to reflect on their progress and to assess the successfulness of the procedures used. He was providing "metacognitive prompts" for awareness of knowledge about problem solving and monitoring of work completed (Lester, 1985:10). Vygotsky's theory of internalization and zone of proximal development, described in *Mind in Society*, is closely related to the regulation part of metacognition (Schoenfeld, 1987, 1992:334-370). In addition, according to Silver (1985), many researchers have been interested in metacognitive skills but labeled them as "control processes" "reflective intelligence," and "executive scheme", etc.

Another predecessor to metacognitive studies was Thorndike's (1917) study of 6th graders' errors in reading paragraphs. He reported that students read passages and failed to monitor their comprehension and even stated that they understood the reading whether they did or did not. He compared the novice students' mistakes in comprehension to the thoughts an expert reader might have while reading. The students would correct their mistakes if they were pointed out, but "they do not, however, of their own accord test their responses by thinking out their subtler or more remote implications" (1917:331).

Thorndike's work on types of courses that improve the ability to think has had an impact on research in areas leading to mathematical cognition (Schoenfeld, 1992:346). He found that effect size of improved thinking was not due to types of courses studied (i.e., mathematics and languages), the then traditional point of view, but that "those who have the most to begin with gain the most during the [school] year" (Thorndike, 1924:95). Good thinkers became better thinkers no matter what subject they studied.

Another area of research that began in the 1950s with the invention of computers—artificial intelligence—refuted importance of the then popular behaviorist movement and renewed study of cognition, focusing on metacognitive skills. Information processing looked at the structure of memory, knowledge representations and retrieval processes, and problem solving rules. In a preface to a collection of edited PhD theses Minsky (1968) defined artificial intelligence as "the science of making machines do things that would require intelligence if done by men". Minsky explained that in order to make non-cognitive computers process cognitive information, researchers had to go beyond the behaviorists' point of view—input-output observables—to mentalists' descriptions of thought processes, which could also be called human cognition skills. This new focus on the importance of human cognition supported the importance of humans reflecting on their cognitive processes (metacognition), but ". . . it was not until the early 1980s that control and other aspects of metacognition began to be a focus of attention for mathematical problem-solving researchers" (Lester, 1994:671). Tulving and Madigan initiated the research field with metacognitive processes in their investigations into human memory (Campione, Brown, & Connell, 1989:93-114) and John H. Flavell (Flavell, Friedrichs, & Hoyt, 1970:324-340) transferred the interest in what humans know about their own memory to what they know about their own cognitive processes. He is credited by many cognitive researchers (Brown, 1987; Campione, Brown, & Connell, 1989; Lester, 1985; Schoenfeld, 1992) as the "Father of Metacognition". His somewhat lengthy description of metacognition is often cited as a starting point for studies in mathematical problem solving (Garofalo & Lester, 1985; Lester, 1985; Schoenfeld, 1985, 1992).

Metacognition refers to one's knowledge concerning one's own cognitive processes and products or anything related to them, e.g., the learning relevant properties of information or data. For example,

I am engaging in metacognition (metamemory, metalearning, metattention, metalanguage, or whatever) if I notice that I am having more trouble learning A than B; if it strikes me that I should double-check C before accepting it as a fact; if it occurs to me that I had better scrutinize each and every alternative in any multiple-choice type task situation before deciding which is the best one; if I become aware that I am not sure what the experimenter really wants me to do; if I sense that I had better make a note of D because I may forget it; if I think asking someone about E to see if I have it right. Such examples could be multiplied endlessly. In any kind of cognitive transactions with the human or nonhuman environment, a variety of information processing activities may go on. Metacognition refers, among other things, to the active monitoring and consequent regulation and orchestration of these processes in relation to the cognitive objects or data on which they bear, usually in the service of some concrete goal or objective (Flavell, 1976:232).

In addition, Flavell (1987) outlined three categories of metacognition with person variables (intra-individual, inter-individual, and global), task variables, and strategy variables. Person variables include information about what we know about ourselves and others when learning. Task variables are knowledge about a specific domain's concepts. And strategy variables are what we know about manipulating domain concepts to answer a question. "Metacognitive knowledge involves the interaction of person, task, and strategy" (Garofalo & Lester, 1985:168). According to Flavell, metacognition is helpful for any organism that thinks a lot; makes mistakes, needing self-regulation to correct; wants to communicate with other organisms; needs to plan ahead; makes decisions; and/or needs to explain phenomena (1987:27). His reflections connect metacognitive problem solving skills to the constructivist learning theory. Both place importance on reflection and critical thinking within the social realm of learning.

Most simply, metacognition is knowing about knowing, and it is most broadly defined as awareness and control of one's cognition (Baker & Brown, 1984; Flavell, 1976, 1987; Gourgey, 2001). As pointed out by Paris and Winograd (1990:7-15), since cognition includes all human mental activities, it is rather difficult to give the notion an operational definition, and researchers emphasize different aspects of it and adopt different terminology all attempting to better illustrate the concept. Flavell (1978, 1987) discussed metacognition from the perspectives of metacognitive knowledge and metacognitive experience, and emphasized the learner's metacognitive knowledge about the variables of person, task and strategy. Brown (1978, 1987) and Baker and Brown (1984) laid more emphasis on the learner's executive control of cognition, including the regulatory activities of planning, monitoring, testing, revising, and evaluating. Paris, Lipson, and Wixson (1983), and Paris and Winograd (1990) proposed self-appraisal and self-management of cognition as two essential features of metacognition (see also Jacob & Paris, 1987:255-278). They described metacognitive knowledge in terms of declarative, procedural, and conditional knowledge; namely, one's cognitive self-appraisal answers questions about "what you know, how you think, and when and why to apply knowledge and strategies" (Paris & Winograd, 1990:17). More recently, Schraw (2001), Schraw and Moshman (1995) defined metacognition as knowledge and regulation of cognition; they divided the former into three kinds of awareness, i.e., declarative, procedural, and conditional knowledge, and focused one's metacognitive regulation on planning, monitoring, and evaluating that help learners control their cognition. I concur with this latest definition and propose three guidelines for EFL writing instruction based on the theories of Paris and Winograd (1990), taking into account all three kinds of metacognitive knowledge and metacognitive regulation.

2.1.2 Metacognition and learning

Metacognitive awareness and self-regulation are of great importance in learning because learners will be able to reflect upon and monitor their cognitive activities, and further develop and employ compensatory and corrective strategies to review and regulate the activities if they are aware of their mental activities. According to Vygotsky (1978), at an early age young children may talk to themselves when encountering difficulties for the purpose of self-guidance and self-direction. The monologues help children reflect on their own behavior and plan alternative actions. As children get older, the self-directed monologues will gradually become internalized as silent, inner speech. Later, researchers have found abundant evidence to support Vygotsky's assumptions and concluded further that the children who talk to themselves, or monitor themselves in terms of metacognition, when facing a challenging task tend to outperform those who do not think about their own cognitive behavior. This cognitive development observed by Vygotsky and other researchers thus lends strong support to the importance of teaching students how to know about and regulate their cognition.

In the last two decades, researchers have attempted to prove that metacognitive learners are beneficial not only in general learning but also in specific subject areas such as reading, writing, mathematics, social studies, and problem solving. They have also attempted to discover the metacognitive knowledge and strategies that students need to be equipped with in order to gain metacognitive awareness and make metacognitive judgments and choices (Baker & Brown, 1984; Brown, 1978, 1987; Gourgey, 2001; Paris & Winograd, 1990; Schraw, 2001). In the field of language learning, Wenden (1998, cited in Zhang, 2003) asserted that learners' metacognitive awareness played a part in the effectiveness of learning.

2.1.3 Scaffolded instruction

Scaffolding is based on Vygotsky's (1978) concept of the zone of proximal development. The concept is

"the distance between actual developmental level as determined by independent problem solving and the level of potential development as determined through problem solving under adult guidance or in collaboration with more capable peers... The zone of proximal development defines those functions that have not yet matured but are in the process of maturation, functions that will mature tomorrow but are currently in an embryonic state".

(Vygotsky, 1978: 86)

In other words, scaffolding involves providing support to students to bridge the gap between what they can do on their own and what they can do with guidance from more competent others including teachers and peers. The reciprocal teaching model, which is developed to teach students reading comprehension strategies, is based upon this concept of scaffolding (Palincsar & Brown, 1989:117-131).

Resenshine and Meister (1992:26-33) identified six basic guidelines for the teachers planning to practice scaffolded instruction: (1) present new cognitive strategies; (2) regulate any difficulties during guided practice; (3) provide varying contexts for students to practice; (4) provide feedback; (5) increase student responsibility; and (6) provide independent practice. Accordingly, at the beginning of teaching students how to perform a new task, the teacher needs to firstly model how to provide the students with complete guidance. The students observe the teacher, an expert model, and do little independent thinking at this point. Afterwards, the teacher provides guided practice in different contexts for the students to practice the strategies modeled in the first step. At this stage, the students attempt to perform the task with the support supplied by the teacher. The support can include the teacher providing additional modeling or thinking aloud, offering hints and feedback, and giving partial solutions. As more guided practice is conducted, the teacher gradually transfers the responsibility to the students by decreasing the amount of support and increasing the students' independent thinking. That is, the teacher's role changes from model to facilitator, and the practice changes from teacher's control to students' self-regulation. Finally, when the strategies are internalized, the students are able to perform the task on their own. Scaffolded instruction is considered effective to develop students' metacognitive knowledge and strategy (Paris and Winograd, 1990:7-15).

2.2 Reading

2.2.1 Defining reading

Though it may be safe to say that the majority of humans are able to read, it may still be misleading since by "the majority" we mean humans acquire the ability of reading with their first language (L1), or native language. As the need of communicating with the others in a foreign language (FL) has become too obvious nowadays, many people are studying one, even two or more foreign languages besides their mother tongue. In this situation, the instruction and research of foreign language, especially English, has been showing their increasing importance. To study EFL reading, it is necessary to give a definition of reading, the basic (of course not the only one) element of human literacy process. In its general sense, reading can be defined as a way to draw information from a text and to form an interpretation of that information (Grabe & Stoller, 2005:4). However the process of reading comprehension is far more complex than this definition has suggested. It may be much more complex when it comes to reading in a second language (L2) or FL, since a reader's L1 acquisition is quite different from his FL learning.

2.2.2 Models of reading

Currently, one of the most prevalent views of reading is interactive processing theory (Swaffar, Arens & Byrnes, 1991:221). The term incorporates two layers of meanings. First, it refers to the interaction between the reader and the text, which means readers consciously build the text meaning with the help of their prior or background knowledge they already have. Therefore, meaning of a text is the result of the interaction or negotiation between readers and the text. Their interpretation of the text is thus highly individualized.

Second, it also refers to the interaction among reading skills. In most cases, reading is the result of interaction between lower-level, bottom-up process skills and higher-level, top-down processing skills (Carrell, 1988b; Eskey & Grabe, 1988;).

Bottom-up theory argues that the reader constructs the text from the smallest units (letters to words to sentences, etc.) and that the process of constructing the text from those small units becomes so automatic that readers are not aware of how it operates (Eskey & Grabe, 1988:191).

Top-down theory argues that readers bring a great deal of

knowledge, expectations, and questions to the text and, given a basic understanding of the vocabulary, they continue to read as long as the text confirms their expectations (Goodman,1967). The top-down process argues that the reader predicts the information in the text with his background knowledge and checks back constantly during the reading process whenever any new information appears and sees that whether or not his prediction is coherent with the new knowledge, in which way comprehension is set up (Eskey & Grabe, 1988:208).

The interactive theory argues that both top-down and bottom-up processes are occurring, either alternatively or simultaneously. The process implies that the reader chooses either or both of the processes to push his comprehension forward. The reader's choice depends on his background knowledge, strategic level, proficiency level, motivation and even cultural-molded beliefs (Eskey & Grabe, 1988:231).

2.2.3 Defining reading strategy

Cohen (1990) defined Reading Strategies are those mental processes that readers consciously choose to use in accomplishing reading tasks. According to this definition, all levels of strategies, from overall, global ones, such as guessing new words from context to more specific ones, like performing, interparagraph analysis to guess words, are all considered "strategies", as opposed to referring to the more specific ones by some other term, such as "technique" or "tactic". Such strategies may or may not facilitate successful comprehension of text. In addition, strategies can be distinguished from skills in that a skill is an overall behavior or general class of behaviors, while a strategy is the specific means for realizing that behavior. For example, skimming would be a skill, while reading the first sentence of each new paragraph would be a strategy for realizing this skill (Cohen, 1990: 83).

"Strategies are those specific attacks that we make on a given problem. They are the moment-by-moment techniques that we employ to solve problems posed by second language input and output."

(Brown 2002: 114)

Brown divided strategies into three main categories.

"Metacognitive strategies involve planning for learning, thinking about the learning process as it is taking place, monitoring of one's production or comprehension, and evaluating learning after an activity is completed. Cognitive strategies are more limited to specific learning tasks and involve more direct manipulation of the learning material itself. Social/affective strategies have to do with social-mediating activity and transacting with others."

(Brown 2002: 115)

2.2.4 The classification of reading strategies

Nunan argued that "by choosing the best strategies for different texts and purposes, it is possible for second language readers to significantly increase both their reading speed and their comprehension" (Nunan, 2001:265-266). A taxonomy of reading strategies is, therefore, commonly conducted by researchers when they carry out researches in reading and its supportive strategies.

Neil J. Anderson (2004) has broken the list of 24 specific reading strategies into the following three different groups:

a) cognitive reading strategies

1. Predicting the content of an upcoming passage or section of the text;

2. Concentrating on grammar to help you understand unfamiliar constructions;

3. Understanding the main idea to help you comprehend the entire reading;

4. Expanding your vocabulary and grammar to help you increase your reading;

5. Guessing the meanings of unfamiliar words or phrases to let you use what you already know about English;

6. Analyzing theme, style, and connections to improve your comprehension;

7. Distinguishing between opinions and facts in your reading;

8. Breaking down larger phrases into smaller parts to help you understand difficult passages;

9. Linking what you know in your first language with words in English;

10. Creating a map or drawing of related ideas to enable you to understand the relationships between words and ideas;

11. Writing a short summary of what you read to help you understand the main ideas;

b) metacognitive reading strategies

12. Setting goals for yourself to help you improve areas that are important to you;

13. Making lists of relevant vocabulary to prepare for new reading;

14. Working with classmates to help you develop your reading skills;

15. Taking opportunities to practice what you already know to keep your progress steady;

16. Evaluating what you have learned and how well you are doing to help you focus your reading;

c) compensating reading strategies

17. Relying on what you already know to improve your reading comprehension;

18. Taking notes to help you recall important details;

19. Trying to remember what you understand from a reading to help you develop better comprehension skill;

20. Reviewing the purpose and tone of a reading passage so you can remember more effectively;

21. Picturing scenes in your mind to help you remember and understand your reading;

22. Reviewing key ideas and details to help you remember;

23. Using physical action to help you remember information you have read;

24. Classifying words into meaningful groups to help you remember them more clearly.

Neil J. Anderson (2004:82-83)

2.2.5 Comprehensible input

Comprehensible input is an idea that originated with Krashen (Krashen, 1981:85). Krashen put forward what he called the input hypothesis, which maintained that

"development from a learner's current stage of L2 or FL learning level, i, to the next stage i+1, is achieved through comprehending language which contains linguistic items at i+1. Comprehension is necessary in order for the input to become intake. The ability to understand new L2 or FL items comes from the speech adjustments made to the learner, plus the learner's use of shared knowledge and context".

(Lasen-Freeman & Long, 1991: 140)

The more lately definition came from several others. According to Ellis (1985), the input refers to the language which learners are exposed to. This can be "comprehensible" (i.e. input that they can understand) or "incomprehensible" (i.e. input that they cannot understand). When native speakers speak to L2 learners, they frequently adjust their speech to make it more comprehensible. Access to comprehensible input may be necessary condition for acquisition to take place. Nunan (1999: 303-304) defines comprehensible input as

"messages addressed to the learner that, while they may contain structures and grammar that are beyond the learner's current competence, and are made understandable by the context in which they are uttered".

(Nunan 1999: 303-304)

According to Krashen's comprehensible input hypothesis, acquisition occurs when learners understand messages that are just beyond their current stage of development. In terms of CALL, Krashen describes optimal input for acquisition as have four characters: "1. it is comprehensible; 2. it is interesting and/or relevant to the acquirer; 3. it is not grammatically sequenced; 4. it is provided in sufficient quality" (Kenning and Kenning, 1990: 87).

2.3 Research on Metacognition Concerning Reading in China

Wen Qiufang (1996) and Yang Xiaohu et al. (2001, 2002) have made their contributions to the studies of metacognition in English teaming and teaching. One thing in common of their research is that these researchers realize the importance of metacognition and argue for the utility of metacognitive theory in reading. For example, in her survey of the relationship between traditional and non-traditional ways of learning and English achievements, Wen Qiufang found that the key to learning effectiveness is students' self-management strategies whose cores are "self-reflection" and "self-evaluation". Successful learners can perceive and adjust the learning behaviors which may result in failures while those unsuccessful learners are less likely to make relevant adjustment even they found that their current learning strategies are of little help (1996:37-42). Here the "self-reflection" and "self-evaluation" show the students' metacognitive level. Wang Wenyu (1998) argues the importance of "management strategies of monitoring and regulation" in her survey of vocabulary learning strategies: among the five memory strategies that significantly correlated with students' vocabulary tests results, management strategies are one of the two variables that of predictability to the results. However, few empirical studies could be seen with regard to integrating the theory to practice. In particular, applying metacognitive monitoring and regulation to reading is left untouched.

2.4 Reciprocal Teaching

Reciprocal teaching is an instructional procedure that features "guided practice in applying simple, concrete strategies to the task of text comprehension" (Brown & Palincsar, 1989:413). Reciprocal teaching was first described by Palincsar and Brown in 1984, and the description was extended in their later articles, particularly in their article in 1989. Reciprocal teaching refers to a set of learning conditions in which children "first experience a particular set of cognitive activities in the presence of experts, and only gradually come to perform these functions by themselves" (Brown & Palincsar, 1989: 123). In reciprocal teaching the focus is upon teaching students specific, concrete, comprehension-fostering strategies which they can apply to the reading of new text, and this instruction takes place primarily in the context of a dialogue between the teacher and the students.

In reciprocal teaching, as developed by Palincsar and Brown (1984), students read a passage of expository material, during which they learn and practice four reading comprehension strategies: generating questions, summarizing, attempting to clarify word meanings or confusing text, and predicting what might appear in the next paragraph.

Palincsar and Brown analyzed the effects of helping young L1 learners with special reading problems by teaching them to monitor comprehension. They called this instruction "Reciprocal Teaching (RT)". It trained the students in the use of four strategies: clarifying, identifying the main idea of a section of text, summarizing, and predicting. During instruction, the teacher modeled the use of each strategy. Then the students were divided into groups and a student was assigned the role of the teacher and modeled the use of these four strategies as they read a text and conducted a group discussion on the use of these strategies. At the end of the instruction, the students were given a comprehension test. According to their study, the experimental group which was exposed to this particular instruction scored higher than the control group which was not exposed to it.

Cotterall (1990) examined Palincsar and Brown's (1984) study in the L2 context. She analyzed the effects of metacognitive strategy instruction on four Japanese and Iranian ESL learners. The findings indicated that the learners benefited from the strategy instruction. Song (1998) also replicated Palincsar and Brown's study in English as a foreign language context and found that strategy training enhanced the reading ability of Korean EFL college learners.

Lysynchuk et al. (1990) carried out a study with grade four and seven poor comprehenders (number = 72) participated in 13 sessions of reading-strategy instruction or reading practice (control condition). Trained students were instructed to make predictions when reading, to generate questions about text, to summarize what was read, and to clarify points that were hard to understand. The strategies were taught using the reciprocal instruction approach developed by Palincsar and Brown (1984), involving provision of support to students as they needed it and peer teaching of strategies. Control subjects were exposed to the same materials as reciprocally trained students but were given no strategy instruction. The most important finding was a greater increase from before to after training on a standardized test of reading comprehension in the reciprocally trained than in the control condition.

In another study, Alfassi (1998) examined whether superiority existed in reciprocal teaching methods over traditional methods. According to the researcher, the purpose of this study was to investigate the effects of strategy instruction on reading comprehension. The main objective of strategy instruction was to foster comprehension monitoring. The study examined whether reciprocal teaching methods (strategy instruction) were superior to traditional methods of remedial reading (skill acquisition) in large high school remedial classes. With a methodology similar to that used in the pioneering work of Palincsar and Brown (1984), 53 students in five reading classes who received strategy instruction were compared to 22 students in three control-group classes. The results indicated that this challenging setting strategy instruction was superior to traditional reading methods in fostering reading comprehension as measured by experimenter-designed reading tests. However, no significant difference was found between the groups on two standardized measures of reading.

Hacker et al. (2002) investigated the implementation and practice of reciprocal teaching in 2 elementary schools. Over a 3-year period, 17 elementary school teachers participated in the implementation of reciprocal teaching. The obstacles they encountered and modifications made to reciprocal teaching were examined. Teachers modified their practice of reciprocal teaching, and the authors examined their modifications using 3 elements of reciprocal teaching: strategy use, dialogue, and scaffold instruction. The focus was on whether these 3 essential elements remained in the teachers' constructions of reciprocal teaching. The authors also focused on whether teachers added anything new to RT. The authors concluded that teachers' practice of reciprocal teaching changed with time, and it changed in response to many variables, and the results at School 2 at the end of Year 3 suggested that the strategic processing that was emphasized had a positive impact on students. The authors also believed that theory and guidelines used to help teachers with the implementation and practice of reciprocal teaching are developed.

Chapter Three

Methodology

3.1 Research Questions

In order to check whether the metacognitive—strategy-based English reading instruction is effective or not, the author conducted an experiment in two contrast groups. The whole program was held in the first term and lasted for 10 weeks. It was designed to check whether metacognitive strategy training would help students to improve their English reading proficiency and efficiency.

On the basis of previous researches and theories, the author hypothesizes that learners' metacognitive levels may account for their reading achievements. That is to say, the effective use of metaeognitive strategies may actively influence learners' reading achievements. There may be some differences in the aspects of reading metacogniton between the students with high scores and those with low scores. Thus, the purpose of this research is to test the effects of metacognitive self-regulation training through reciprocal teaching on learners' reading strategy use. This study is to answer two questions:

Does reciprocal teaching of English reading produce more positive effects on reading strategy use than the teaching without self-regulation training? If so, what specific reading strategies can this reading instruction help students to use more freely and automatically?

3.2 Subjects

The subjects involved in the study were 120 students from grade two of Zhaotong Experimental Middle School. They were given the pre-test, and based on their marks and data analysis derived from the independent samples t test via Statistical Package for Social Scienle(SPSS) 10.0, they were divided into two groups, the controlled group and the target group. The purpose of the test and analysis was to ensure the general level of English reading proficiency of the two groups had not significant difference ($p>0.05$). In other words, their English reading competence was at the same level (see table 3.1 & 3.2).

Table 3.1 The comparison of means between the target group and the controlled group

Group	Number	Mean	Std. Deviation	Std. Error Mean
The controlled group	60	63.7333	9.10926	1.17600
The target group	60	65.5333	8.34727	1.07763

Table 3.2 The t-test for equality of means

	t-test for Equality of Means				
	t	df	Sig. (2-tailed)	Mean Difference	Std. Error Difference
Equal variances assumed	-1.128	118	0.261	-1.80000	1.59507
Equal variances not assumed	-1.128	117.111	0.261	-1.80000	1.59507

3.3 Instruments

3.3.1 Questionnaire

To test the instructional effect, a questionnaire (see Appendix 1) was given and translated into Chinese to students in the two groups to find out their habitual employment of various reading strategies during the instruction or in the post-test after it. The questionnaire was adapted and translated into Chinese from the self-report Reading Strategy Questionnaire (RSQ) employed by Ikeda and Takeuchi (2000). Some items were reworded to make it more suitable for Chinese EFL context. The questionnaire was composed of 23 reading strategy items, and responses were recorded using a Likert scale of 1 (almost never) to 5 (almost always) (see Appendix 1 for detail).

These questionnaire items were concerned with metacognitive, cognitive and social/affective reading strategies that were closely related to the actual reading process (see Table 3.3).

Table 3.3 Taxonomy of reading strategies in the questionnaire

	Variable	Item number	Percentage (%)
Meta-cognitive	Pre-planning and arranging	2, 11, 19	13.0
	Self-monitoring	4, 5	13.0
	Selective attention	14	4.3
	Problem-identification	16	4.3
	Directed attention	17	4.3
Total items	8		34.8
Cognitive	Predicting	1, 7	8.7
	Repetition	18	4.3
	Translation	20	4.3
	Skipping	12, 15	8.7
	Identifying main ideas	6	4.3
	Inferencing	10	4.3
	Summarizing	21	4.3
	Guessing	8, 9	8.7
	Underlining	13	4.3
Total items	12		52.2
Social/affective	Cooperation	22, 23	8.7
	Self-reinforcement	3	4.3
Total items	3		13.0

3.3.2 Experimental tests

Two reading comprehension tests—pre-test and post-test—were conducted to obtain students' reading comprehension scores. All of the reading passages and their comprehension questions of the tests are taken from National English Proficiency Competition for Secondary School Students (NEPCS). The test tools are 100 multiple-choice reading questions.

The pre-test consists of four reading passages. And the 50 questions in the pre-test are grouped as: five main idea questions, twenty-five factual or detailed questions, ten global inference questions, and ten word attack questions. In the end, a question "Have you ever read one or more of the above passages?" is attached to the reading passages in order to guarantee the credibility and validity of the survey. Those who have read any of the passages will be tested by other test passages, which they have not read before.

Another four passages of similar type are provided as the post-test after training, and the 50 questions in the post-test are grouped as: five main idea questions, twenty-five factual or detailed questions, ten global inference questions, and ten word attack questions. In the end, a question "Have you ever read one or more of the above passages?" is attached to the reading passages in order to guarantee the credibility and validity of the survey. Those who have read any of the passages will be tested by other test passages, which they have not read before.

The total score is 100 points. The time is confined to 45 minutes.

3.4 Methods

This empirical study was carried out on 120 students from grade two of Zhaotong Experimental Junior Middle School. They were divided into two classes: one was treated as the target group (number = 60), and the other was the controlled group (number = 60). They had the same English teacher, and the target group receives reading instruction by using the "Reciprocal Teaching" method (Palincsar and Brown, 1984) for 10 weeks and the controlled group receives the reading instruction without reciprocal teaching. Although the earlier studies (Palincsar and Brown, 1984; Carrel et al., 1989; Alfassi, 1998; Hacker et al., 2002, etc.) reported that the combined effects of metacognitive and cognitive strategy instruction were effective in enhancing reading comprehension in either L1 context, L2 or EFL context, the present research tends to investigate the effects of the same instruction practice on junior middle school students' reading strategy by using Chinese context.

3.5 Procedures

This study can be divided into three stages. The first stage lasted for one week (the first week) to pre-test the students, grouped them and gave the target group necessary training to use reciprocal teaching. The second stage was from the second week to the ninth week for reading instruction. For each week, two sessions' teaching was given to both groups. The first two-hour session was devoted to teacher-guided instruction, while for the second two-hour session, the first hour was used for students-modeled group learning with teacher's assistance and direction and the second hour was given for "office hour", during which the teacher gave students pre-scheduled group tutorial to answer students' questions, record their feedback on the instructions and their reading strategy use. And the other students not interviewed were required to finish their assignments within groups. It is understood here that the teacher consulted the students from both groups, and teacher's feedback given to the students was in line with the holistic teaching objectives, procedures and the underlying rationales for the two models of teaching. The third stage was the tenth week, during which a questionnaire was filled out and a post-test was given. Then the relative data were analyzed.

3.5.1 Taking pre-test

At this stage, one session was devoted to giving the pre-test to the subjects. After the session, the test papers were marked, and the marks were typed into an SPSS file. Then the independent samples test was performed for the tentative groups until the difference between the two groups was small enough to be insignificant. Another session was used to introduce how to carry out reciprocal teaching to the students, while the introduction of different reading strategies was given to the controlled group.

3.5.2 Instructions with two models

The second phase was from the second week to the ninth week. The controlled group received reading instruction without reciprocal teaching, while the target group was taught reading with self-regulation training through reciprocal teaching. They were going to finish studying two units within eight weeks. The main teaching objectives for both groups were to raise their awareness of using reading strategy, to improve their reading performance and help them use some effective reading strategies freely and successfully.

3.5.3 Taking post-test and filling in questionnaire

The third phase was the tenth week, during which the two groups were firstly given a post-test to investigate their mastery of reading strategies. After that, they were required to fill in a questionnaire to investigate their self-reflection on reading strategy use after the instruction.

3.5.4 Data collection and analysis

The rest of the tenth week was used to mark the post-test and collect the questionnaire data. Then the statistical analysis software SPSS version 10.0 was employed to perform the independent samples t test. A significance level of .05 was set in this research. The independent samples t-test was utilized to compare groups of test-takers (including means and standard deviation to determine t-value), and to find out whether the difference between the two groups in strategy using was significant or not.

Chapter Four

Experimental Instruction

In this chapter, a detailed description of the first four-week instruction (two sessions of 4 hours in each week) is given, since the rest four-week instruction repeat the same instructional procedure. As mentioned above, this instruction was supposed to finish two units. The difference is that the target group studied the units with reciprocal teaching, while the controlled group without the training. Both groups were taught by the same teacher.

It was noted that when finishing the first four weeks of learning, both groups got more familiar with the teaching procedure and the relevant requirements. They were well prepared for their study of the second unit during the next four weeks. In order to describe the procedure more clearly, the first four-week instruction, i.e. from the second to the fifth week, was reported in detail in this section. And it is understood that the second four weeks' instruction follows the same procedure, and more importantly, more satisfactory effect was gained since the same instruction procedure was repeated for a second time. The teaching objectives were designed as follows: by the end of the instruction, students should be able to:

Be aware of the importance of strategies use while reading and employing their schema knowledge to enhance their reading comprehension;

Use their schema knowledge consciously to facilitate their reading comprehension process;

Use such reading strategies as skimming for main ideas, scanning for important information, predicting text content, monitoring comprehension, and guessing word meaning from context.

4.1 Instruction to the Controlled Group

To the controlled group, a traditional model of reading instruction for four weeks was given, during which students were supposed to finish learning a passage named "Living in the Outback" (see Appendix 2). The instruction mainly went through the following steps:

The first session for each week.

Week Two

(1) The students and the teacher looked at the title of the selected text and made predictions about the likely content of the passage, based on the title. The teacher encouraged students to activate their background knowledge related to the content of the text. Worksheets were distributed to the students. The teacher asked students to write down anything that he she believed to be related to the topic and if necessary, he/she could write down words

or sentences in Chinese and consult dictionary for the English. After finishing it, the teacher asked students to share what they have written down with their partners beside them and explain to each other the meanings.

(2) The class was divided into six groups with 10 students in each group. Before they started reading the passage, the teacher read the first paragraph and demonstrated how to (a) summarize and find the main ideas in that paragraph, (b) predict what will come next, and (c) seek clarification of any comprehension difficulties. At this stage, some repair strategies were introduced to the students such as re-reading problematic parts, reading on until the meaning became clear, using the context to guess the meaning of unknown words, visualizing the content in the text, and asking the teacher or friends for help.

Week Three

The teacher assigned each group to read one paragraph of the text. One of the students in each group volunteered or was asked to become group leader and followed the procedure described. The teacher observed each group and provided further explanations about the procedures and/or use of strategies and encouraged students to take part in the activity.

Week Four

In this session, each group nominated a representative to report the main idea of what he/she has read and other students acted as a judge, an information provider or an evaluator. After each groups' report, the second round of discussion started when each group commented other groups' prediction of the main idea of the paragraph they was assigned to read. During the whole session, students could speak in Chinese if they could not explain their idea clearly in English. After the discussion, the teacher summarized each group's performance in their comprehension correctness and the suitability of strategy use.

Week Five

After the text was finished, the whole class discussed the main ideas together. The teacher especially encouraged students to relate the content of the text to their personal experiences, and students were allowed to speak in Chinese if they were asked to do so to make it easier for them to participate in the discussion.

The second session for each week.

As to the second session for each week, the teacher led the class to read another text named, "Mind your Manners" (see Appendix 3), finish the exercises, answered students' questions and gave feedbacks to students' homework.

4.2 Instruction to the Target Group

To the target group, an experimental model of reading instruction was given, during which students were supposed to finish learning the same passages as the controlled group. The instruction followed the procedure of reciprocal teaching.

The first session for each week.

Week Two

This session dealt with pre-reading tasks and was divided into

3 stages.

At the first stage, the teacher divided students into 6 groups with 10 students in each group. The teacher asked students to discuss and note down any information on Nicky on their worksheets. Then group one was required to present their findings, after which the teacher summarized the presentation. The purpose for the task was to activate students' content schema. The strategies having been trained was speaking skill of sharing information with each other.

At the second stage, the teacher presented the task of "vocabulary study" and listed the words, "outback, Internet, and vacation " on the blackboard. He asked students to explain the meaning of these words, and asked students to define the word according to word formation rules and reminded students not to use a dictionary. Then students of group two present their work to the class. The teacher summarized the presentation and the reading strategy of guessing word meaning from available clues was used. The purposes for this task were to activate students' linguistic schema, to provide students with a chance to try top-down learning process and try to help them build up their confidence of this learning process, to build up students' confidence of using top-down learning process, to cultivate group collaboration and to raise students awareness of meta cognitive knowledge of reading strategies. The strategy focused at this stage was to deduce word meaning according to the morphological clues—word formation.

At the third stage, the teacher summarized the text and assigned homework for the next week.

Week Three

This session dealt with pre-reading tasks and was divided into 3 stages.

At the first stage, the teacher asked students to predict what the passage was about according to the title. Then the teacher asked students to discuss it in groups and group three was asked to present their prediction to the whole class. The teacher did not correct students and told them that they can check the correctness of the prediction later. The teacher summarized the reading strategy of predicting passage content according to available clues such as the picture in the textbook. The purposes for this stage were to activate students' content schema, to practice the reading strategy of predicting reading content and to raise students' awareness of metacognitive knowledge of reading strategies. The strategy focused on content predicting according to the title.

At the second stage, the teacher asked students to go on with a vocabulary task—semantic mapping (Assumption: this type of activity has been carried out since the beginning of the semester) and write down as many words relative to the manners in different place as possible on the worksheet and told students that they could use their dictionary if necessary. Then the teacher stopped the students and asked students of group four to present their work to the whole class. After that the teacher asked students to group the words and used a more general word to categorize each group. For the time sake, each group was required to compose at most three groups with four words in each group. The teacher asked students of group four to present their result to the whole class on computer. The purposes for this stage were to help students foster the metacognitive knowledge of reading strategies use, to activate students' linguistic schema and to direct students to use top-down processing to work with relevant vocabulary. The strategy focused on top-down processing of vocabulary building.

At the third stage, the teacher summarized the relative reading strategy to raise students' awareness of metacognitive knowledge of vocabulary study strategies.

Week Four

This session dealt with while-reading tasks and was divided into 3 stages.

At the first stage, the teacher wrote down fast reading questions on the blackboard and asked them to go over the questions before reading. After that the teacher asked students to read the article quickly and finish both reading and question-answering within 3 minutes. Then the teacher checked the answers with students and reinforced the ways of doing skimming and scanning. The purposes for this stage was to form prediction before reading, to do skimming and scanning and to foster students' metacognitive knowledge of reading strategies use in reading. The strategies focused on skimming and scanning at this stage.

At the second stage, the teacher asked students to put the text aside and join with another group to form three larger groups. Then the teacher showed his/her division of the passage into four parts and assigned each group to finish reading one part of the passage within their group. Firstly, the teacher read the first part to the students and demonstrated how to (a) summarize and find the main ideas in that paragraph, (b) predict what will come next, and (c) seek clarification of any comprehension difficulties. Meanwhile, some repair strategies were introduced to the students such as re-reading problematic parts, reading on until the meaning becomes clear, using the context to guess the meaning of unknown words, visualizing the event in the text, and asking the teacher or friends for help. After that, the teacher asked students to read and discuss the part together intensively to make sure that they were all satisfied that they understood it and could explain it to others including the vocabulary in it. Then he asked each group to write down two questions about the content of the rest of the text on their worksheets. Here the teacher should help students to come up with more clear and specified questions so that the other groups may know what it refers to. Finally, the teacher asked students to form new groups with other two students who had read the rest parts and told the others one by one the main idea of his/her part. The purposes of performing this jigsaw reading task were to create information-gap to activate students' content schema knowledge and motivate them to predict the content of the rest of the reading based on their own part and to practice the reading strategy of predicting and checking. The strategies focused at this stage were content predicting, question writing, spoken skill of explaining and questioning, summarizing the main idea with students' own words and content sequencing or ordering.

At the third stage, the teacher summarized the relative reading strategy to raise students' awareness of metacognitive knowledge of vocabulary study strategies.

Week Five

This session dealt with post-reading tasks and was divided into 2 stages.

At the first stage, the teacher asked students to reread the passage and make a list of the main events mentioned in the passage and write it down on the worksheets. Then he asked group five and six to present their results to the whole class. At last, the teacher summarized what students had learnt from the passage.

At the second stage, the teacher evaluated the performance of the six groups according to the files made during study and his/her personal observation and asked the best group to make a presentation on the topic of "How we have used reading strategies to help comprehend a passage". Then he summarizes the whole session.

The second session for each week.

Student-modeled group learning.

From the second week to the fifth week, students may have one hour in each week to model their teacher's instruction during the first session to raise their awareness of English reading process and their metacognitive knowledge about reading strategy use according to the reciprocal teaching. During this hour, students worked in their group. They were supposed to repeat what they had gone through during the first session with a new passage, "Living in the Outback". The teacher assigned one paragraph for each group and asked a group leader to perform the role of teacher and lead the group to repeat what they have done in the first session. When group work began, the teacher walked around to give necessary direction and assistance. For the following week, the same procedure was followed with another group leader and a new paragraph till they finished learning the whole passage in the fifth week session. Then teacher summarized student performance during the group learning and the reading strategy use involved while reading.

The office hour.

The group tutorial, nevertheless, was the same as that given to the controlled groups, during which the students reported their questions concerned with the text study such as vocabulary, difficult sentences and grammar points, understanding about others' oral presentation and the problem about strategy use, and doubts about others' prediction. Students also reported their awareness of strategy use.

Chapter Five

Data Analysis and Result

At the end of the study, data were collected through recording the test marks and tallying the questionnaire choices. This chapter gave detailed analyses and discussions on the causal factors of the analyzed results and the implication of the results on future teaching practice.

5.1 Analysis of the Pre-test and Discussion on the Results

5.1.1 Analysis of the pre-test

The purpose for arranging the pre-test is to ensure that the subjects divided into two groups are generally at the same level of English proficiency. In accordance with this purpose, 120 subjects were chosen randomly and arranged to take a placement test of English reading. All of the reading passages and their comprehension questions of the tests were taken from National English Proficiency Competition for Secondary School Students

(NEPCS). The test papers were marked immediately after the test and the marks of the subjects were recorded. Then the subjects were divided into two groups based on the Independent Samples t-test results carried out by using statistical software SPSS 10.0 to ensure that the means of the two groups show no significant difference. The result was given in the following table 5.1.

Table 5.1 T-test for difference between two groups in the pre-test

	t-test for Equality of Means				
	t	df	Sig. (2-tailed)	Mean Difference	Std. Error Difference
Equal variances assumed	-1.128	118	0.261	-1.80000	1.59507
Equal variances not assumed	-1.128	117.111	0.261	-1.80000	1.59507

Independent samples t-test is utilized to examine the results of the pre-test of the two groups. As shown in Table 5.1, there is no significant difference between the two groups at 95% level ($p>0.05$). That is to say, the reading competence of the two groups was almost at the same level in the pre-test.

5.1.2 Discussion

Recent studies on language learning strategy findings suggested that L2 strategy use was associated with English proficiency level and it was believed that students of higher proficiency used strategies more successfully than lower ones. Dreyer and Oxford (1996) reported a correlation of .73 between English proficiency scores and strategy use for university ESL learners in South Africa, while Oxford and Ehrman (1995) found a correlation of .61 between proficiency and strategy use for adult foreign language learners. Other strategy inventory for language learning studies have shown lower but still significant correlations between strategy use and L2 proficiency: .35 in Thailand (Mullins, 1992), .30 in Japan (Watanabe, 1990), and .26 in Korea (Park, 1994). Taken together, these results suggested rather consistently positive relationships, ranging from mild to strong, between strategy use and L2 proficiency. However, for the present research, what was tested was the effect of computer-mediated reading instruction (v.s. traditional classroom reading instruction) on reading strategy use. Therefore, it is crucial to restrict the proficiency variable and make sure that students start at the same level.

5.2 Analysis of the Questionnaire and Discussion on the Results

After eight-week instruction, a questionnaire was given to the subjects. The purpose was to find out whether or not the application of reciprocal teaching brought some positive effects on reading strategy training, and whether there were some strategies which could be trained more effectively through reading instruction with reciprocal teaching than through traditional classroom teaching practice without it. 120 copies of the questionnaire papers were handed out to both groups of students, who were asked to finish it in class. Then, the questionnaire papers were collected. The questionnaire data were coded and put into computer for statistical analysis to answer the research questions indicated above. Thanks to teachers' careful preparation and detailed explanation of how to fill in the questionnaire correctly, all the 120 copies of the questionnaire were considered acceptable for statistical analysis.

Descriptive statistics (means, standard deviation, etc.) were employed to obtain information about different uses of listed reading strategies used by the controlled and the target groups. To determine significance throughout the study, the author of this study assigned the p value at the level of .05. This means that a result is considered statically significant if it can occur by chance fewer than 5 times out of 100.

5.2.1 Analysis of the general means of the two groups

The questionnaire was designed and modified on the basis of the self-report Reading Strategy Questionnaire (RSQ) employed by Ikeda and Takeuchi (2000) in conformity with the actual situation of the school where the research took place. As for the reading strategy use in the questionnaire, two sets of data were collected and analyzed. The first was general mean scores based on the 23 reading strategies. The second was the mean scores related to each strategy used by both groups.

Table 5.2 T-test of the mean difference between groups concerning general use of reading strategies

	Controlled Group	Target Group	t	df	Sig. (2-tailed)
Mean	2.9870	3.1406	1.789	44	0.080
SD	0.3759	0.1682			

The results of Table 5.2 indicated that although the mean scores of the target group was higher than that of the controlled group (3.1406 vs. 2.9870) in reading strategy use, the difference was not significant (p>.05). Therefore, no significant difference between the two groups was found as far as the general use of reading strategies was concerned, which meant that computer-mediated reading instruction did bring some positive effects on reading strategy use than traditional classroom instruction of English reading, but the difference was not statistically significant enough.

5.2.2 Analysis of the means of each questionnaire item

But significant difference did occur between the two groups in using some individual strategies, which are Items 1, 2, 8, 9, 10, 13, 16, 17, 18, 22 & 23.

The difference of using meta-cognitive reading strategies (Items 16 and 17).

As indicated in table 5.2, the students' employment of certain metacognitive strategies between the two groups was significantly different (p<.05). In other words, the target group reported to use these metacognitive strategies more frequently and successfully than the controlled group (Item 16: I would like to read the comprehension questions first before I read a passage. Item 17: If I have some questions of understanding, I go back to read the previous paragraphs to get a better understanding).

The difference of using cognitive reading strategies (Items 1, 8,

9, 10, 13, and 18).

Moreover, more cognitive reading strategies were used differently between the two groups. The controlled group outperformed the target group significantly in using Item 9: whenever I met some new words, I consulted a dictionary to find the meaning ($p<.01$) and the difference was very significant. And very significant difference was also found in Item 8—when coming across new words, I guess their meaning according to the context ($p<.01$); Item 10—I can work out the implied meaning of a sentence from the surface meaning ($p<.01$); Item 13—I underline important sentences in a passage ($p<.01$) and Item 18—I can choose the appropriate reading strategies, such as skimming and scanning, to aid my comprehension ($p<.01$). Still there was one significant difference in using strategy 1—I make use of the title of a passage to help predict the main idea of it ($p<.05$). For these strategies, the target group reported more frequent and successful use than the controlled group.

The difference of using social and affective reading strategies (Items 22 and 23).

In using social and affective reading strategies, significant difference was found between the two groups. For Item 22—I would like to discuss anything that I cannot understand in a passage, the target group reported more frequent employment than the controlled group ($p<.05$), while for Item 23—I like to check my understanding of a passage with others, the same result was found ($p<.05$) (see Table 5.3 for detail).

Table 5.3 Differences between the target group and the controlled group in the use of individual strategies

Strategy	Target Group		Controlled Group		t	Sig. (2-tailed)
	Mean	SD	Mean	SD		
1	3.0000	0.7878	2.4000	1.0034	2.576	0.013*
2	3.3000	0.8367	2.7667	0.8976	2.381	0.021*
3	3.0000	0.7428	2.9000	0.8847	0.474	0.637
4	2.9667	0.7649	2.9333	0.7849	0.167	0.868
5	3.0000	0.6433	3.1000	0.6618	-.593	0.555
6	3.1333	0.7761	3.4667	0.7303	-1.713	0.092
7	3.0667	0.7849	3.3333	0.7112	-1.379	0.173
8	3.3333	0.6609	2.8667	0.6814	2.693	0.009**
9	3.2333	0.6261	3.9000	0.8847	-3.369	0.001**
10	3.3333	0.8023	2.7333	0.7397	3.012	0.004**
11	3.0667	0.8277	3.2667	0.5208	-1.120	0.267
12	3.0000	0.8305	2.7667	0.8584	1.070	0.289
13	3.0333	0.8087	2.2667	0.8683	3.539	0.001**
14	3.0333	0.8087	3.3667	0.7649	-1.640	0.106
15	3.1000	0.6618	3.3000	0.5960	-1.230	0.224
16	3.4667	0.7303	2.9667	0.7649	2.590	0.012*
17	3.1333	0.8193	2.6000	0.8137	2.530	0.014*
18	3.0000	0.6433	2.4667	0.7761	2.898	0.005**
19	3.2667	0.8683	3.2333	0.8584	0.150	0.882
20	2.8000	0.8469	3.1333	0.8604	-1.512	0.136
21	3.2333	0.5683	3.1333	0.5713	0.680	0.499
22	3.3667	0.8503	2.8667	0.5713	2.673	0.010*
23	3.3667	0.8087	2.9333	0.6915	2.231	0.030*

* $p<0.05$

** $p<0.01$

5.2.3 Discussion

From the above data analysis, we can find that the overall result was mixed in that although no significant difference was found in students' overall reading strategy employment between the target group and the controlled group, some significant differences were really found in using certain strategies. This finding supported some earlier studies (Gore et al., 1989; Arroyo, 1992).

The reasons for the overall insignificance between the two groups may be that, firstly, eight-week instruction is not long enough for significant difference; secondly, there may exist deficiency in the present design of reciprocal teaching, which incorporates only a few reading strategy instruction materials and the presentation of them is also problematic, since only a few silent hypertext in flash format are given to introduce reading strategies at the beginning of each reading session. This findings support a similar survey made by Kleinmann (1987). In his study, no significant difference was found in score gain between the experimental group and the control group. He attributed the results to poor software programs used and strongly argued that it was important to create more innovative reading software programs that could foster more interaction between a student and a computer and could provide activities for enhancing reading comprehension skills and strategies based on a solid understanding of L2 reading. These findings, in this sense, provide directions for further research in the future in this area.

Discussion of significant difference in using certain

metacognitive strategies (Items 16 and 17).

For using some metacognitive strategies, the target group reported more frequent use of Items 16 and 17, which may be due to more collaboration work done by the target group and the effective modeling through the reciprocal teaching. As mentioned, reciprocal teaching can promote collaboration. With the advantages, collaboration may happen naturally in this environment, while in traditional classroom teaching, teacher-centered instruction is predominant and students are unlikely to collaborate more often unless an explicit direction is given by the teacher. And among collaborative groups in the target class, the reciprocal teaching can facilitate students to learn more knowledge from both the teacher and their peers. The high performers in reading may reflect their study process verbally and share their reflection with the rest group members. Even the students with lower reading proficiency may find that they can also play a leading role with their other expertise, for example, their information on Sherlock Holmes. The reading instruction given in the traditional context, on the other hand, is much more limited by students' teacher-dependence, and the teacher-centeredness (which left students with little chance to display their unique competence. Therefore, it is very hard to establish mutual trust and dependence among the students), and the lack of resources, especially at students' end. Consequently, it may even take them longer to learn to use the reading strategies.

According to Burley's finding, metacognition tends to improve with age and develop more adequately with proper instruction

(1985). The instruction to the target group is designed to promote students' strategy use and activate their metacognitive knowledge. Again with successful collaboration and the effective reciprocal modeling, students' metacognition was activated more successfully in computer-mediated learning environment than that in a traditional classroom, where although the teacher taught explicitly the same strategies to the controlled group, the lack of peer interaction and collaboration may cause the students to take longer time to internalize the way of using the strategies.

The effective use of metacognitive strategies like redirecting attention and changing original plan accordingly supported Dreyer et al.'s finding (2003).

Discussion of significant difference in using certain cognitive strategies (Item 1, 8, 9, 10, 13 and 18).

For these six items of cognitive reading strategies listed in the questionnaire, the target group reported more use of 5 items than the controlled group, and the differences between the two groups were significant. Among them the differences on four items (Items 8, 10, 13 and 18) are very significant ($p<.01$). The main reason for the result was perhaps that reading instruction with reciprocal teaching might enable the students to use reading strategies more effectively than traditional classroom teaching practice. As mentioned earlier, peer collaboration is an important feature of reciprocal teaching. Through collaboration, students shared their understanding of teachers' instruction, and of the learning material with each other more often than the controlled group students. They also worked together to negotiate the meanings of reading passages and to finish the tasks assigned by the teacher. In this case, they got more chances to practice the reading strategies, to experience success and failure in strategy use, to retrospect and review what they had learned by far and to correct any mistakes appeared.

Interestingly, the controlled group reported a significant difference over the target group on Item 9. This might result from the effect of the bottom-up way of reading on this part of students. They would like to consult a dictionary anytime when they meet a new word. And it also indicated the lack of effectiveness of instructing the top-down strategies in traditional classroom reading instruction.

The effective use of cognitive strategy of predicting before and while reading also supported Dreyer et al.'s finding (2003).

Discussion of significant difference in using certain social strategies (Items 22 and 23).

The significant difference in using social strategies (Items 22 and 23) between the two groups revealed the fundamental difference existing between reciprocal teaching and traditional classroom teaching. For the traditional classroom teaching, the teacher is the center, authority and the only resource of the classroom reading. Students depend heavily on their teachers for knowledge, strategy and feedbacks. As a result, little attention is paid to collaboration among students. There is an evident lack of trust of other's command of English among students. Therefore, when problem occurs, students may only turn to their teacher for help. However, during reciprocal teaching, students need to be self-autonomous in their study. The teacher plays the roles of supervisor, organizer, mediator, facilitator and consultant, etc. This teaching environment is student-centered, since tasks were assigned to every group of students to finish together. And some students find that their self-assumed advantages over their peers in English study may be counteracted by their disadvantages in other aspects, such as background knowledge. In this case, a call for collaboration is initiated as the needs to share each others' expertise become more and more evident. However, although the needs of collaboration have been fostered in students' mind, teachers, especially in Chinese context where teachers are considered as an absolute authority in the classroom, have to legitimize this learning mode with explicit requirements. From the present research, it was found that students in the target group collaborated much better and more consciously and spontaneously than those in the controlled group. When the study started, the teacher made a clear direction that they need to form small groups within which an English "expert" and an information "expert" must be identified for future study and consultation. This counteraction of learning powers is crucial for students to establish their confidence, motivation and sense of achievements.

The effective use of social strategy of cooperation was also reported by Feng and Cui (2006) when studying the effect of computer-assisted language instruction in the Chinese EFL context.

5.3 Analysis of the Post-test and Discussion on the Results

5.3.1 Analysis of the difference between the two groups in the post-test

After the eight-week training, the two groups took part in the same post-test of reading comprehension. The type of this test was similar to the pre-test. All of the reading passages and their comprehension questions of the tests were taken from National English Proficiency Competition for Secondary School Students (NEPCS). Table 5.4 presents the results.

Table 5.4 T-test for difference between two groups in the post-test

	Controlled Group	Target Group	t	df	Sig. (2-tailed)
Mean	66.100	68.967	-1.800	118	0.074

The independent samples t-test was used to examine the results of the post-test of the two groups. As shown in Table 5.4, although the target group achieved a higher mark than the controlled group (68.967 v.s. 66.100), there was not a significant difference between the controlled group and the target group in their reading performance in the post-test (p>.05), which means that there is not a significant difference at 95% level.

5.3.2 Discussion

As the data analysis shown in this section, computer-mediated reading instruction did bring some positive effect to the target group students but this overall effect was not statistically significant. The possible reasons are discussed as follows:

Firstly, as mentioned above the design of reciprocal teaching needed improving to incorporate more effective and interactive activities that were capable of motivating students to get themselves involved in more reading strategy trainings. And the activities also needed being accompanied by explicitly instruction, which could enrich students' metacognitive knowledge and experience of reading strategy employment.

Secondly, studies suggest that good strategy use is complex and thus calls for prolonged and detailed instruction (Pressley et al., 1989) and "both the first language and the second language research literature on reading strategy training which involves emphasis on some or all of the five metacognitive elements (what, how- to-use, why, when and where, and evaluation) has clearly shown that such teaching can definitely make a difference in the short term, but metacognitive reading strategy teaching should also be a long term educational process, with constant attention and support over longer periods of time" (Carrel, 1998).

Therefore, although the computer-mediated instruction produced different and positive outcomes for the target group students, it might be the limited length of time assigned to the instruction that made the improvement over the controlled group not significant enough.

This finding is consistent with the earlier findings of Kleinmann (1987) and Hamilton (1995). It also supports Alfassi (1998)'s finding in that no significant difference was found from the results of standardized test.

5.3.3 Analysis of the difference in some individual comprehension items between the two groups

Although overall significant difference was not verified with the post-test result, some significant difference was really discovered when we compared the performance of the scores of each comprehension item between the two groups. The purpose for the analysis was to find whether there was significant difference between the two groups in some items which tested students' ability of using specific reading strategies. To realize this purpose, all the comprehension items were chosen for detailed analysis. The marks of these items were collected and calculated within each group. And the results are presented as follows.

Table 5.5 The comparison of the mean scores of specific items between the two groups

	Group	N	Mean	Std. Deviation	Std. Error Mean
Inferring	control	60	14.0667	1.73564	0.22407
	target	60	14.1000	1.70443	0.22004
Vocabulary	control	60	13.5833	1.55456	0.20069
	target	60	14.2000	1.79264	0.23143
Main ideas	control	60	7.4000	0.92425	0.11932
	target	60	7.4000	0.99490	0.12844
Specific information	control	60	31.0500	6.92924	0.89456
	target	60	33.2667	4.71516	0.60873

Table 5.6 The T-test of means difference of specific comprehension items between the two group

		t-test for Equality of Means		
		t	df	Sig. (2-tailed)
Inferring	Equal variances assumed	-0.106	118	0.916
	Equal variances not assumed	-0.106	117.961	0.916
Vocabulary	Equal variances assumed	-2.013	118	0.046*
	Equal variances not assumed	-2.013	115.683	0.046*
Main ideas	Equal variances assumed	0.000	118	1.000
	Equal variances not assumed	0.000	117.365	1.000
Specific information	Equal variances assumed	-2.049	118	0.043*
	Equal variances not assumed	-2.049	103.992	0.043*

* $p<.05$

As shown in the table 5.6, there is not significant difference in students' answering main idea questions ($p>.05$), and actually the two groups got the same mean score in dealing with this type of comprehension questions. Table 5.6 also indicates that in dealing with the items that check students' ability of guessing the meaning of a new word from the context, students in two groups did show significant difference ($p<.05$). This means that students of target group performed significantly better than the controlled group after the eight-week reading strategy training with reciprocal teaching. Once again, students in the target group achieved higher marks, which verifies that there was a significant difference in using relevant reading strategies to help them find the answers to the questions about specific information in a passage ($p<.05$). And in dealing with inferring questions, there was no significant difference between the two groups (p>.05).

5.3.4 Discussion

This section of analysis has found that significant difference appeared when students used the strategy of guessing word meaning from the context and scanning for specific information. The target group did significantly better in using these strategies, which might be due to the different models employed in the two groups during reading instruction. From the implementation section, we could find that the controlled group followed the traditional model of reading instruction, while the target group followed the interactive model and emphasized more use of top-down strategies, for example, the teacher encouraged students to predict the content with the help of their schema knowledge, to scan for some important information and to guess word meanings from the context. All these practices enabled student to get familiar with the strategy, to take a try and to get successful experiences. When the students had verified the effectiveness of these strategies, they tended to have a second and third try until the use of them become automatic.

More importantly, with the assistance of reciprocal teaching and the teacher's explicit directions, students were motivated effectively to try these strategies while read the text shown on the computer screen. Most of the time they had to work with their group peers to work out the meaning and construct their comprehension. As a result, they got more time of practice than the controlled group students who listened to the teacher's elaboration most of the time.

The finding that reading strategy instruction with reciprocal teaching is effective in training students to acquire such strategies as guessing word meanings form the context and scanning for specific information is consistent with some earlier researches (Wise and Olson, 1994; McKenna, Reinking, Labbo and Watkins, 1996; Lange, 1999; & Konishi, 2003, etc.)

5.4 Pedagogical Implication

As discussed above, the insignificant difference found in both the questionnaire investigation and post-test between the two groups might be due to the short period of time allotted for the training. But the researcher of the present study believes that the more important reason is that students' metacognitive knowledge about reading strategy use has not been fostered completely. Therefore, it is advisable that the teaching of reading strategy should include not only the cognitive knowledge about strategies, i.e. "I know what the strategies are", but also the metacognitive knowledge about them, i.e. "I know what, how, why, when and where to apply those strategies and I can assess whether the application is effective or not". And the teaching of reading strategy should be planned and carried out systematically and explicitly and over a long period of time. As for computer mediated instruction of reading strategy, a designer should consider how to integrate more interactive activities that can enable collaboration and negotiation of meanings into the courseware, and how to design more activities that are capable of allocating different tasks to group members who are good at them and motivating students to collaborate to solve problems and fulfill the tasks. With these well-designed tasks, and during their interaction, discussion and negotiation of them, students can exchange, clarify, internalize and reinforce the reading strategies involved.

The significant findings imply that firstly, the teaching of reading strategies needs to be contextualized. But that does not mean merely writing down some examples on the blackboard, and illustrate how to use certain reading strategies. Anderson concluded from his data that successful second language reading comprehension was

"not only a matter of knowing what strategy to use, but the reader must also know how to use it successfully and know how to orchestrate its use with other strategies. It is not sufficient to know about strategies, but a reader must also be able to apply them strategically". (Anderson, 1991: 468-469)

Similarly, Kern (1997) concluded from his data that "there were good and bad uses of the same strategy, and that the difference between a 'good' use and a 'bad' use of the same strategy was in the context in which they were used, how they were used and how they interacted with other strategies." In other words, Kern says, "the difference is how the strategies are 'operationalized'" (Carrell, P. L., 1998).

In classroom teaching, teachers should also be aware and prepared in teaching reading strategies with more metacognitive supports. It is important to know the strategies and how to use them, but it is equally important for students to know where, when, why to use them and to be capable of evaluating the effects of strategy use.

As for the reading strategy instruction with reciprocal teaching, teachers should make good use of its functions to construct contexts for strategy instruction. Teachers should also provide students with enough chance to operate what they have learned and to experience both success and failure in strategy use, which helps to perfect students' metacognitive knowledge about strategy use. And teaching designers should take all-round consideration about these conditions and collaborate with classroom teachers to better the design of reciprocal teaching. Only when the underlying rationale from the two sides matches perfectly, can reciprocal language teaching produce effective results.

Chapter Six

Conclusion

    This book reports an empirical study, which examine the effects of a trial mode of reading instruction with reciprocal teaching on students reading strategy use.

    It was found that the overall reflection of strategy use among readers was mixed in, although no significant difference was found in students' overall reading strategy employment between the target group and the controlled group after experimental instruction, but some significant differences were really found in using certain strategies. They were the metacognitive strategies of problem-direction (I would like to read the comprehension questions first before I read a passage) and directed-attention (If I have some questions of understanding, I go back to read the previous paragraphs to get a better understanding); cognitive strategies of predicting (I make use of the title of a passage to predict the main idea), guessing (when coming across new words, I guess their meaning according to the context), inferencing (I can work out the implied meaning of a sentence from the surface meaning), underlining

(I underline important sentences in a passage) and repetition (I can choose the appropriate reading strategies, such as skimming and scanning, to aid my comprehension); and social strategies of cooperation (I would like to discuss anything that I cannot understand in a passage, and I like to check my understanding of a passage with others). For the above strategies, the target group reported more frequent use than the controlled group. However, the controlled group did report more frequent use of strategy of consulting a dictionary for word meaning.

It was also found that although reading instruction with reciprocal teaching brought some positive effects to the target group on their use of reading strategies and their test performance, the difference was not statistically significant enough. However, the analysis of the scores of some typical comprehension questions found that the target group got significant higher mark than the controlled group. The strategies included guessing word meanings from the context and scanning for specific information. This finding shows that reading instruction with reciprocal teaching really enhances students' awareness of reading strategy employment and the use of some strategies has become automatic in solving comprehension problems.

There are limitations of this research. Firstly, only 120 subjects were chosen in the experiment, and the small samples might affect the results of this experiment. Secondly, the questionnaire concerned was not comprehensive enough to encompass all elements of metacognitive strategies, just because of the complication of the students' use of metacognitive strategies. At last, due to the limitations in time, the author did not provide enough contexts for the employment of strategy and the tasks were insufficiently designed to cultivate students' metacognitive knowledge about reading strategies.

In spite of the limitations which are mentioned above, the present study, in some way, inspires the teachers and the researchers to explore continuously for the future study on the use of metacognitive strategies in English reading. First, if the condition is permitted, more subjects should be added to this kind of empirical studies, and the conclusion of the experiments will be more convincing. Second, if the time permits, the future research should undertake a long-term training in order to observe the improvement of students' reading comprehension during the training process and examine how to improve their effective use of metacognitive strategies. Finally, further research methodologies of comprehension monitoring are needed to be explored experimentally, which have demonstrated value for improving students' reading ability.

Some suggestions were also made to the future teaching. First, teachers should integrate more tasks of fostering students' metacognitive knowledge on strategy use into their instruction. Second, the author calls for bettered design of reciprocal teaching, which should incorporate more contextualized tasks and more interactive functions into it to facilitate students' reading strategy use.

Based on the above research and its findings, the research concludes that reading instruction with reciprocal teaching method do produce some positive effects on students' strategy use, and such strategies as guessing word meaning from the context and scanning for specific information are successfully internalized after the instruction. Meanwhile, students' awareness of strategy use while reading is enhanced and the collaboration is successfully realized among these students.

However, owing to the short experimental period of time and small size of students, these findings still need to be verified in the future research. The author also suggests that more research needed to investigate metacognitive knowledge cultivation and its effects on reading strategy use in junior middle school EFL learning environment.

References

[1] ALFASSI M. Reading for meaning: The efficacy of reciprocal teaching in fostering reading comprehension in high school students in remedial reading classes [J]. American Educational Research Journal, 1998, 35 (2): 309-332.

[2] BAKER L, BROWN A L. Metacognitive skills and reading[J]. Handbook of reading research, 1984: 353-393.

[3] BROWN A L, PALINCSAR A S. Knowing, learning, and instruction: Essays in honor of Robert Glaser [M]. New York : Routledge, 1989.

[4] BROWN A. Metacognition, executive control, self-regulation, and other more mysterious mechanisms [J]. Metacognition, motivation, and understanding, 1987: 65-111.

[5] CARRELL P L. Interactive Text Processing: Implications for ESL/Second Language Reading Classrooms[M]. Cambridge: Cambridge University Press.1988.

[6] CARRELL P L, PHARIS B G, LIBERTO J C. (1989). Metacognitive strategy training for ESL reading [J]. TESOL Quarterly, 1989, 23(4): 647-678.

[7] COHEN A D. Language Learning: Insights for learners, teachers, and researchers [M]. New York: Newbury House/ Harper Row, 1990.

[8] COTTERALL S. Developing Reading Strategies through Small Group Interaction [J]. RELC Journal, 1990, 21(2): 55-59.

[9] ESKEY D E, GRABE W. Interactive Models for Second Language Reading: Perspectives on Instruction. Cambridge: Cambridge University Press. 1988.

[10] FLAVELL J H, FRIEDRICHS A G, HOYT J D. Developmental changes in memorization processes[J]. Cognitive Psychology, 1970, 1: 324-340.

[11] GRABE W, F L STOLLER. Teaching and Researching Reading [M]. Beijing: Foreign Language Teaching and Research Press, 2005.

[12] ROBERT M GAGNE. Instructional Technology: Foundation [M]. New York: Routledge, 1987.

[13] GAROFALO J, LESTER F K JR. Metacognition, cognitive monitoring, and mathematical performance [J]. Journal for Research in Mathematics Education, 1985, 16: 163-176.

[14] GOODMAN K. The Reading Process: Interactive Approaches to Second Language Reading [M]. Cambridge: Cambridge University Press, 1975.

[15] GOURGEY A. Metacognition in learning and instruction [M]. The Netherlands: Kluwer Academic, 2001.

[16] GU YONGQI, JOHNSO R K. Vocabulary learning strategies and language learning outcomes [J]. Language Learning, 1996, 46: 643-679.

[17] JACOBS J E, PARIS S G. Children's metacognition about reading: Issues in definition, measurement, and instruction[J].

Educational Psychologist, 1987, 22: 255-278.

[18]　KENNING M M, KENNING M J. Computers and language learning: current theory and practice [M]. New York: Ellis Horwood, 1990.

[19]　E A Silver. Teaching and learning mathematical problem solving: Multiple research perspectives [M]. Hillsdale, NJ: Lawrence Erlbaum, 1985.

[20]　Krashen S. Second Language Acquisition and Second Language Learning [M]. Oxford: Oxford University Press. 1981.

[21]　LARSEN-FREEMAN D, M LONG. An Introduction to Second Language Acquisition Research [M]. New York: Addison Wesley Longman Inc. 1991.

[22]　LESTER F K JR. Musing about problem-solving research: 1970-1994 [J]. Journal of Research in Mathematics Education, 1994, 25: 671.

[23]　MINSKY M. Semantic information processing [M]. Cambridge, MA: The MIT Press. 1968.

[24]　NEIL J ANDERSON. Exploring Second Language Reading[M]. Beijing: Foreign Language Teaching and Research Press, 2004.

[25]　NUNAN D. Second Language Teaching and Learning[M]. Boston, MA: Heinle & Heinle Publishers, 1999.

[26]　NUNAN D. Second Language Teaching and Learning[M]. Beijing: Foreign Language and Research Press, 2001.

[27]　PALINCSAR A, BROWN A. Reciprocal teaching of comprehension-fostering and comprehension—monitoring activities [J]. Cognition and Instruction, 1984, 1: 117-175.

[28] Paris S G, Lipson M Y, Wixon K. Becoming a strategic reader[J]. Contemporary Educational Psychology, 1983, 8: 293-316.

[29] Paris S, Winograd P. Promoting metacognition and motivation of exceptional children [J]. Remedial and Special Education, 1990, 11(6): 7-15.

[30] PÓLYA G. How to solve it: A new aspect of mathematical method [M]. 2nd ed. Garden City, NY: Doubleday Anchor Books, 1957.

[31] ROSENSHINE B, MEISTER C. The use of scaffolds for teaching high cognitive strategies [J]. Educational Leadership, 1992, 49(7): 26-33.

[32] SCHOENFELD A H. Learning to think mathematically: problem solving, metacognition and sence marking in mathematics[J]. Handbook of Research on Mathematics Teaching and Learning, 1992: 334-370.

[33] SCHRAW G. Current themes and future directions in epistemological research [J]. A Commentary Educational Psychology Review, 2001, 13(4): 451.

[34] SCHRAW G, MOSHMAN D. Metacognitive theories[J]. Educational Psychology Review, 1995, 7: 351-373.

[35] SWAFFAR J, ARENS K, BYRNES H. Reading for meaning: an integrated approach to language learning[M]. Englewood Cliffs, NJ: Prentice Hall, 1991.

[36] THORNDIKE E L. Reading as reasoning: A study of mistakes in paragraph reading [J]. The Journal of Educational Psychology, 1917, 8(6): 323-332.

[37] THORNDIKE E L. Mental discipline in high school studies[J]. The Journal of Educational Psychology, 1924, 15: 95.

[38] VYGOTSKY L S. Mind in society [M]. Cambridge, MA: Harvard University Press, 1978.

[39] WEN Q, JOHNSON R K. L2 learner variables and English achievement: A study of tertiary-level English majors in China[J]. Applied Linguistics, 1997, 18: 27-48.

[40] ZHANG L J. Awareness in reading: EFL students' metacognitive knowledge of reading strategies in an input-poor environment[J]. Language Awareness, 2001, 11 (4): 268-288.

[41] NEIL J ANDERSON. 第二语言阅读探索：问题与策略[M]. 北京：外语教学与研究出版, 2004.

[42] 文秋芳. 英语学习策略论[M]. 上海：上海外语教学出版社, 1996.

[43] 杨小虎, 张文鹏. 元认知与中国大学生英语阅读理解相关研究[J]. 外语教学与研究, 2002(3).

Appendix 1

Reading Strategy Questionnaire

Name: Sex: Number: Class:

Directions: Show how often you use the strategy when reading, 1 means "never", 2 means "occasionally", 3 means "not sure", 4 means "often", and 5 means "always".

(   ) 1. I make use of the title of a passage to predict the main idea of it.

(   ) 2. I make a reading program to ensure that I can do a lot of reading.

(   ) 3. I become much more self-confident in my reading with the improvement of my reading skills.

(   ) 4. In the reading process, I constantly adjust my understanding according to the context, verifying the prediction.

(   ) 5. While reading, I always read the questions first, then decide which method to choose—scanning, skimming or else.

(   ) 6. I browse the article first in order to get the main idea.

(   ) 7. While reading, I predict the following content according to the information that have been mentioned.

(　　) 8. When coming across new words, I guess their meaning according to the context.

(　　) 9. Whenever I met some new words, I consulted a dictionary to find the meaning.

(　　) 10. I can work out the implied meaning of a sentence from the surface meaning.

(　　) 11. I always consider what type of text it is, such as a newspaper article or a scientific one.

(　　) 12. I skip when reading, so that I can get the important information.

(　　) 13. I underline important sentences in a passage.

(　　) 14. While reading, I pay attention to the headline, small title and the topic sentence of each paragraph.

(　　) 15. In order to get the main idea of an article, I skip the less important information.

(　　) 16. I would like to read the comprehension questions first before I read a passage.

(　　) 17. If I have some questions of understanding, I go back to read the previous paragraphs to get a better understanding.

(　　) 18. I can choose the appropriate reading strategies, such as skimming and scanning, to aid my comprehension.

(　　) 19. In order to improve the reading ability, I pay attention to background knowledge learning.

(　　) 20. In order to understand some sentences better, sometimes I analyse and translate them.

(   ) 21. I would like to summarize my every period of study.

(   ) 22. I would like to discuss anything that I cannot understand in a passage.

(   ) 23. I like to check my understanding of a passage with others.

Appendix 2

Living in the Outback

Nicky Logan is 13 year old , and she comes from the Australian Outback. She lives on a farm with her parents, her brothers Martin and Ben, and 50,000 sheep.

The Logan's farm is in the "Outback". A lot of Australia is "Outback"—it's very hot and dry, and not many people live there. Sometimes Nicky and her family don't see any other people for weeks.

So how do Nicky and her brothers go to school? Well, they don't go to school—their school comes to them, by radio and the Internet. They sit at home and talk to their teachers and classmates on the radio. Their classmates live on other farms and their teachers work at the "School of the Air", in a place called Alice Springs. When the pupils have to do homework, they sent it to their teachers by fax or the Internet.

When Nicky isn't studying, she likes to ride her horse and help the farm workers with the sheep. It's hard work for a young girl, but she enjoys it. Sometimes she plays tennis with her brothers, and when it's very hot, she likes to go swimming in the river on the farm.

"I really like living on an outback farm," says Nicky. "There are very cool animals like koalas and kangaroos. But not all the animals are cool. There are some dangerous snakes and spiders here. They can be scary!"

The "School of the Air" is only for younger students. So next year, when Nicky is 14, she has to go to a school in Alice Springs. She is going to live at the school and visit her family during the vacation. "I'm going to miss my parents and my horse," she says, "but I still want to go, I want to study with other kids for a change."

Appendix 3

Mind your Manners

Around the world, people have different ideas about what good table manners are. In India, for example, people only eat with their right hands. You take food from one dish on the table, usually a kind of bread or rice, mix it with food from another dish and then put it in your mouth. Your left hand stays still. Eating with your left hand is very rude!

In western countries, people don't usually share the same dishes. Everyone has his or her own plate of food. You eat with a knife and fork and you shouldn't wave them around when you aren't eating. And you should try not to be noisy when eating. People think that's bad table manners!

When you go to restaurant in different parts of the world, it's important to know what people think is rude. For example, in China it's OK to be noisy in a restaurant. In fact, if a restaurant isn't noisy, you may think it's not very good. However, in many western countries, restaurants are quiet places. If a table is too noisy, other customers might not be happy.

Paying for the meal is also different from country to country. In

China, one person usually pays for everyone. In western countries, when friends eat together, they usually share the cost. This is called "going Dutch". Also, when westerners pay the check, they usually leave some money for the waiter. This is called "leaving a tip". Not leaving a tip is very rude. In the U.S., it's common to leave tips of 10%, 15%, or 20% of the check. The amount depends on how good the waiter was. Good waiters can get a lot of money.

  The way people eat food is different around the world, but you can find same kinds of food in many countries. Chinese and Italian food, for example, are popular all over the world.

Postscript

It took me more than one year to write this book. This book could not be finished without the help and support of many people who are acknowledged here.

First and foremost, I would like to express my sincere and deepest gratitude to my supervisor, professor Yang Bingjun, whose patient and meticulous guidance and invaluable suggestions were indispensable in the process of my dissertation writing when I studied in Southeast University, for this book was written mainly based on the dissertation. Without his profound knowledge, constructive suggestions and active encouragement, I could not have completed this book.

My sincere thanks also go to Professor Wen Xu, Professor Li Li, Professor Chen Zhi'an, Professor Liu Yu and other teachers whose excellent lectures and insightful suggestions have helped me lay the foundation to compose this book when I was studying in School of Language, Southwest University.

I would like to express my gratitude to my dear friends, who have given me so many suggestions and helped me a lot in the process of data collection and data analysis. I also owe my sincere gratitude to my friends and my fellow classmates for they have encouraged me and given me suggestions when I had problems and was lost in writing this book.

Last but not least, I would like to thank my family members for their support, encouragement and loving consideration. It is their love, support and encouragement that helped me overcome all kinds of difficulties in the past years.